BOOKS BY DARYL HINE

POETRY

Minutes   1968

The Wooden Horse   1965

The Devil's Picture Book   1961

The Carnal and the Crane   1957

Five Poems   1954

FICTION

The Prince of Darkness and Co.   1961

TRAVEL

Polish Subtitles   1962

MINUTES

MINUTES

Poems by Daryl Hine

New York   Atheneum   *1968*

ACKNOWLEDGMENTS: Some of these poems have appeared in the following periodicals: *The Atlantic Monthly, The Malahat Review, The New York Review of Books, The New York Times, Partisan Review, TriQuarterly*

FOR SAMUEL TODES
AND
IN MEMORY OF ANTONY STERN

MINUTES

When first I saw you on the viewing-screen
I wondered what you were doing: in your hand
You held a new kind of machine, its moving parts,
Like the imprinted heart of a calculator,
Turned, and you took pleasure in their turning;
And these, you said, are the minutes that I am reading.

MINUTES

THE WREATH

*The François vase, in the Louvre, is envisaged. The
story is told in Bacchylides' 17th Dithyramb, how
Theseus, accompanying the last shipment of victims to
Crete and challenged by Minos to prove that Poseidon
was his father, dived into the sea and was received in an
underwater palace by Amphytrite, who gave him a
wreath of unwithering roses.*

Are they setting foot
Ashore, or are they getting
On? Is it the end
Of a premeditated voyage
Or is it the beginning?
Muse, do we recognize
Among the pleasure-seekers
One to whom virtue
Once was an alternative?
I do not know who knows,

Save that one by one
The tenses are exploited,
Time itself is made
Slave to a different employment
As by a godlike labour
That could not be put off:
The something of the present
Painfully altered
To a picture of the past
Where anyone may see

As in a rear-view mirror
What he imagines best
About that other world. So

It is not possible to tell the colours of the flowers.
The porpoises that leap among the waves
Lead secret lives, shyly conspicuous.
Skill is a tyrant over seem and be.
Whose wedding chamber was a watery tomb?
Which silken shirt became a sheet of flame?
For these are only two such accidents, of many
That I could show, if it were not for time.

There was a marine wreath, a garland of unwithered roses . . .
Here they are now, forever dry and bright
Since they belonged to one who shall be nameless
From whose bones the city borrowed flesh.
Their shape is banished from the frivolous limbs
Of all the judge's victims, I mean time's,
Long since, of that half thrilled, half apprehensive cargo
Of once pubescent boys and nervous nymphs

Sentenced to be transported
With him, like Theseus,
Aboard the good ship Venus

To a terrible triumph.
Où voulez-vous aller?
The vessel is of silver,
Upon a gilded sea,
The youths and maidens are
Of lapis lazuli.

They have nothing to tell us.
Each masterpiece outlasts
The secret of its meaning
As if it ever had
A meaning. As he surfaced,
Round the ocean rang,
There crept across the water
In their wake a music
Of unutterable voices.

4

The Survivors   42

Farewell to the Point   43

Tableau Vivant   45

Lovers of the River   46

Among Islands   49

The Nap   51

CONTENTS

The Wreath   3

Lady Sara Bunbury Sacrificing to the Graces   5

The Apology   6

Natasha's Letter Scene   9

Foreign Parts   11

Les Yeux de la Tête   12

The *Marché aux Puces* and the *Jardin des Plantes*   13

Le Rendezvous des Gourmets   14

Clôture Annuelle   15

Flavigny-sur-Ozerain   16

Dans le Marais   17

Envoi   18

His Longing for Paris (George Buchanan: *Desiderium Lutetiae*)   19

Noon   23

The Copper Beech   24

Song   26

Total Immersion   27

The Trout   28

August 13, 1966   30

A Conceit   31

A Visit   32

Untitled   35

Point Grey   37

Terminal Conversation   38

A Present   41

LADY SARA BUNBURY SACRIFICING TO THE GRACES, BY REYNOLDS

The perfect dear whom no one blames
For her good luck and looks and breeding
Breathes from the canvas. Reynolds frames
Her in a temple, reading.

What is the book? As Sara's pale
Attention wanders from the page
Her fingers stroke the print like braille,
Her eyes engage.

Good at games? Beside her see
On a convenient pedestal
Palette and lute and embroidery,
All testimonial

To her skill in every art to which
A Bunbury may condescend,
As one of the Muses—who knows which?
Or just a friend,

A cousin, it might be, of the Graces
To whom she addresses her sacrifice:
Handsome girls with oval faces,
Straight noses and nice

Manners. Her rivals. A dainty yawn
Dimples the priestess' delicate chin.
Remark in dance on the shaven lawn
Rustics, Death and Sin.

THE APOLOGY

The time machine at last has broken down
Acknowledging that all it knows are lies.

At last? But did it ever really fool
Us with its manufactured memories?
The feeling that we'd seen this bit before
With younger actors and a cleverer routine?
And this is dull. Who can sufficiently deplore
The hackwork hallucination the machine
Does best, like the description of the town
Where, say ten years ago, one went to school?

Was it a lion, a lily or a woman?
Broken, reluctant figures of something else
In the stairway window where the sunlight dyed
Pale, spotty faces, every feature false.

But what in that should make the clockwork stop
When at their worst the works run in reverse
Fetching the reader back from last to first
Impressions at the regular rate of verse?
Because the poem works like a machine,
Like the machine perhaps, it runs on rhyme
Garbling the syllables between,
(An antiquated model? There's no time
For invention!) and consuming drop by drop
Salt, sperm, tears, blood, sleep, hunger, and thirst.

For more than one have learned to walk on knives,
Believing that the only way to walk
At seventeen, and some go sailing in a sieve
In momentary terror of the clock.
But over the abyss of bygone days
Inch by inch and sick with vertigo
We must advance blindfold, forbidden to gaze

Backwards: never, never glance below!
There are so many minutes in our lives
And not one second hand in which to live.

These, immaturity, were your miracles
And, thaumaturgic muse of the Romantics!
These your great and lesser vehicles,
Fiction and the folly of semantics.
You followed language careless where it went
To final, all but metrical collapse.

One sees in you the adolescent who
Once answered to the kiss refused
By one he didn't really want to kiss,
"This mouth, rebuked too often, will be used
For other work than kisses." Blasphemy!
As if language were a substitute
For love! And worse to come: he said, "Let me
Rehearse in places where I should be mute
What others in silence and discomfort do."

So what? was the secret of experience,
Unnatural, by nature meaningless,
That brought about a breakdown in the works,
A stained glass window whence in fancy dress
A myth stepped down at midday to confess
To a funny business no one had accused
Of mystery——the very words I used
To put you in your place with accidents
Where between dream and doing meaning lurks.

Ma pauvre belle, I wish I could be plain.

Many mouth obscenities in hope
That thereby the parts of speech will mate.

The muse washed out this poet's mouth with soap;
Now when I speak out of my frothy lips
Portentous bubbles float, and in my wake,
Like *obiter dicta* in the comic strips.
The air is burdened with them; as they break
They glitter, worlds within words and without weight,
The nightingale's mechanical refrain.

NATASHA'S LETTER SCENE

Nothing works, not the evening at Uncle's,
The sleighride or the gypsies; he is gone
Away, not here, absent, lost, elsewhere,

And though he writes long, interesting letters
Full of advice and affectionate admonition,
I do not see his face between the lines

As it were the face of a prisoner,
Looking out of the barred window of his prison,
Imprisoned but still himself and thus still free,

And I cannot quite believe the signature
At the bottom of the final page, *André*.
What is he doing in the Caucasus?

When will he come? Why is he not here?
The sleighbells in the frosty air seem to announce him,
And the stranger stamping in the hall, dressed like a bear.

A hundred times an hour I run to the window:
The drive is empty, last night's snow unbroken;
Downstairs it is only Nastasya, the fool, dressed like a bear.

On New Year's Eve we visited the neighbours
In fancy dress, and I as a hussar
With cork mustaches; I danced like one possessed.

Perhaps I am possessed? What demon do they
Say possesses girls of seventeen?
Why doesn't he come? He should be here

Now. Then we told our fortunes in the mirror.
It is said if you look obliquely in the mirror
On New Year's Eve, and if you are lucky,

You will see the features of your future husband.
I looked and looked, and I could see nothing,
But Sonya said that she saw—him

Lying under a rose-coloured quilt. "Don't you see him?
Why is he?—What does it mean? His eyes are open."
I looked again. The mirror too was empty.

Love and death live very close together
Like neighbours, and I think they pay
Each other visits, sometimes, in fancy dress.

Why else did he want me to be free?
Why did he insist we wait a year
When all this time we might have been together?

Today the footman brings another letter
Inscribed in his handsome, distant hand:
"For the Countess Rostova, dear Natasha."

FOREIGN PARTS

The traveller shrinks in the midst of his journey.
The white sail dwindles upon the grey sea,
The figure on the mountain pass grows smaller,
Minute the voyager on the one-vistaed plain;
The airplane winks and vanishes.

The traveller shrinks in the midst of his journey
After a certain point by distance determined,
Unable to react, describe, return,
Diminished by details, at every turn
Unwilling to wish or make a decision.

The traveller shrinks in the midst of his journey
And coming at night to the imagined inn
Finds foot and rest and perhaps an adventure,
Where everything is different from at home,
And he will register under a strange name,
If there is room and they will let him in.

The traveller shrinks in the midst of his journey.
I picture you leaving
A city I know and cannot see you arriving
In another where I have never been.
O yes, the tourist changes with each change of scene,
Sinking to the guidebook on his knee
Or swelling till his conscience fills, smaller and clearer,
The rear-view mirror.

The traveller shrinks in the midst of his journey.
As one grows older,
Pregnant with pity, one cannot hope to shoulder
The burdens born to others every day.
Other rhymes, nearer, dearer, colder, and beholder
Hint melodiously, misleadingly at what I want to say.

LES YEUX DE LA TÊTE

As exercises in a foreign measure
To the ear or on the page may seem the same,
And does it matter, so the sound give pleasure?
I haunt the district under another name,
A tourist returned, sadly misdirected
By memory to the historic spot where
Once nothing happened, dark glasses reflecting
The pedestrian sun's indifferent glare.

I wear for my variety of reasons
The uniform disguise of a time and place
As much mine as anyone's. In all seasons
Lenses of necessity disgrace my face.
I grope for affection, glaucopic lover,
In bed or thinking I want to go to bed,
Blind when best to be seen. Now night shades cover
Beauties that cost, they say, the eyes of the head.

Why not? The eye is first of all a mirror,
Though not of the soul. On its bright surface swim
Whole argosies of joys. Least speaking feature,
Its objects see in it what it sees in them:
A tiny palace and a formal garden
In miniature, lawns, flowers, jewelled trees
By Fabergé, and in the midst a fountain
Whose precious drops like tear drops fill the eyes.

THE MARCHÉ AUX PUCES AND THE
JARDIN DES PLANTES

The sight of beauty simply makes us sick:
There are too many hours in the day,
Too many wicked faces built like flowers
And far too many bargains for a song.
Jade and paste, cashmere and ormolu—
Who said that all the arts aspire to music?
It's obvious, for time is obvious,
That all that art aspires to is junk.

Blackmailed by these mathoms of the past,
One is indebted for another perspective
To quaint giraffes and quainter wallabies,
The nearly human and the faintly monstrous,
The outrageously contemporary joke.
Trespassing on a no man's territory,
Unlike the moralist one is at a loss
Where to be human is not to be at home.

In a zoo, you see, one can acquire nothing:
Zebras aren't wishes. Nor is the flea market
Exactly the place for those who know what they want.
Like far out stations on the Metro (which they are)
Somewhere, in heaven perhaps, they correspond,
In the heaven of open arms and unpaid bills,
Where beer is drunk on the lawn all afternoon
And every night we bid, and make, a slam.

LE RENDEZVOUS DES GOURMETS

The price is fixed, the courses foreordained,
Hors d'oeuvres, the soup of the day, unvarying vegetable;
Choice is limited to the inevitable
Crudities, what you call *delicatessen*,
The eternal hard-boiled egg . . . If you complain
The quality is always much the same,
Well, apart from physical pain and heartbreak
Our daily bread is dull, but it sustains us.

Then the main course, which tends to come too soon:
Steak or chicken, fried or boiled potatoes.
For those whom the doctor, disgust or conscience make
Vegetarian there is salad or plain noodles
And afterwards cheese, custard or an apple.
From egg to apple all has been too much,
Simple rations but in a tasteless profusion.
What one does twice a day if one is lucky,

What no one really likes to do alone,
Wine and love can make a celebration.
Thus every meal might be a sacrament
Once established, not only a last supper,
But a last breakfast, lunch and tea.
As often as one raised his glass or passed the mustard,
One might say—you or I might say, "As often
As you do this, do it in remembrance of me."

CLÔTURE ANNUELLE

X in August: I should not have forgotten,
I ought to have guessed that it would be so awful,
Empty, monotonous as a month of Sundays,
Yet haunted somehow like a monument
To it would be easy to say I don't know what,
Except I do: to all the other Augusts,
Equally hot or unequally overcast,
Last year and the year before the last,

When I waited, which I wasted waiting,
Wondering what else to do with time but waste it,
For the long, chaste summer to be done with, the beginning
Of intimate autumn and the promiscuous winter.
I am of those who never go away,
All the more rare, then, to find myself a stranger
In streets I thought I knew by heart, but where
The shuttered shops alone return my stare.

Life leers from every terrace and embrasure,
Tricky, inaccessible and dear.
In mid-off-season time is a temptation.
Invaders occupy the café tables
Where in the Spring we spoke to one another.
How wise you were, my dear, to go elsewhere.
Today it is clear. Search me. Our sources give
The oracle's hermetic answer, "Live!"

FLAVIGNY-SUR-OZERAIN

Trees that drink the darkness up like sponges,
Birds that leave their twittering in the branches,
Once vocal birds as voiceless now as fishes,
Discreet as bats that flit from shade to shade.
Are there ears that hear the high pitched voices?
Feet that do not stumble in the darkness?
Lucid eyes that contemplate the valley?
Senses to comprehend the valley's shape?

The village sleeps or it pretends to sleep
Behind its shutters, tired with the moon
Who in her final quarter climbs the sky,
And like a smile her light explores the streets
Where nothing moves except a silent cat.
Safe as houses, convents, barns and churches!
Safe! as in the shadow of the ramparts
We watch the valley from the valley gate.

Strange to think how this was Caesar's camp.
Here were campfires, standards, challenges,
Passwords couched in unimaginable Latin
And dispatches in sub-ciceronian prose:
"On the opposite hilltop Vercingetorix
Waits, praying perhaps to the moon goddess
To get him out of this fix. Caesar tonight
Expects the end of her empire and of his."

DANS LE MARAIS

How wise you were, my dear, to go elsewhere,
Your native country or another shore,
The landscape of the olive and the vine,
Incredibly green valleys where everything is green,
The market places and the holy places,
Museums, too, where all the masterpieces
Were genuine. So you, learning a new language,
Escaped from the imaginary voyage.

I have sat as in a darkened room,
My interest else-and-every-where.
An adolescent in the Old Folks' Home
Is not more ill at ease than I am here
And now, dreaming of travel, knowing I can't
Endure its privations even in advance.
I start from nothing and reside at once,
Love, and feel that it is impotent.

But you abide, whether near or far,
Familiar and unutterably odd,
In the abyss or merely on the brink
Of love, perfect and preposterous.
And having no idea where you are,
Addressing you is like addressing God:
To think
That you were one of us!

ENVOI

The ship is in the harbour, the fish are in the sea,
The wind is in the sails, the tide is in, and we
Are indisposed to travel, we prefer dry land,
The false, familiar face, the disappointing hand
To the stranger's clumsy touch and speculative stare.

Can you hear them singing, singing high up in the air,
The over-subtle sirens, like sphinxes, with one voice
Secretively suggesting, "Man must make a choice.
Home is heaven and forgiveness. Abroad is simply hell.
Who would choose the ocean to inhabit, and the bitter swell?"

HIS LONGING FOR PARIS

(George Buchanan: DESIDERIUM LUTETIAE)

Handsome Amaryllis: already now the seventh winter,
Seventh summer detain me far from sight of you;
But neither winter rough with clouds of snow
Nor winter glowing with consuming fires
Has quenched the cares that wake within my heart.
You are my song every morning when
The cattle browse upon the dewy fields,
You my song beneath the blaze of noonday,
And when nightfall stretches out long shadows,
Night, who seals up everything in darkness,
Cannot hide your face from me: in darkest
Night I speak to you and take you in my arms,
And in the unreal seeming of a dream
Fleeting joys caress my careful mind.
Sleep goes and cares are born again with light;
In my unhappiness I flee the house
As if it held the seeds of discontent,
And grieving amid the solitary fields
Wander wherever vagrant error leads,
Wearying unfrequented caves and woods
And sympathetic stones with my laments.
Echo alone, pitying my groans, returns
Groan for groan and plaint for plaint, and often
As I draw sighs up from my heart she sighs
Too in answer from a neighbouring cave.

Sometimes on some sheer pinnacle of high
Precipice, gazing forth upon the sea,
Raving, I address the dark blue foaming
Billows, and cast vain vows to the deaf blasts:
"O sea, and you Nereids who cleave
The glassy waves of the sea, becalmed admit me
To your safe harbours home. Or if this
Be too much to ask, I do not refuse

To go as a castaway so long as I
Am cast away on those beloved shores."
How often have I said to West winds blowing
In your direction, "O, you happy breezes
Who soon will breathe upon fair Amaryllis!
So be it the Pyrenees on their rough slopes
Ground not your wings, nor clouds break off your course.
Tell Amaryllis of Daphnis' furious flame."
How often I addressed the East wind as
With light wings it grazed the level deep:
"Fortunate you, who have seen Amaryllis:
Tell me, does she remember me, and does she feel
Our wound as well? Are there vestiges
Living of that ancient flame of ours?"
But the wind, ungentle, with a rising howl
Flies off as if enraged, and then my heart
Frost-bitten, freezes, and heavy languor seizes
Fast my lifeless limbs. The consolations
Of a shepherd's life cannot divert me now,
Not shepherds' pipes nor the lightfooted bands
Of nymphs dancing in the meadows, nor
The songs goat-footed satyrs harmonize;
Amaryllis alone has rapt away my love.

Lycisca, gifted in drawing music from the rattling
Tambourine, and soft Melaenis loved me,
Spanish girls, both in the flower of youth,
Both rich and proud. Both their fathers had
Promised me as dowry a hundred lambs
With their mother ewes, and in secrecy
Their mothers too had pledged me gifts of money.
But neither their money nor their snow-white lambs
And ewes could influence my heart at all:
No, not all the dainty delights the tender maids
Made me. For, as far as Spring

Surpasses Winter, or a wholesome boy
A man stricken in years, or the full-grown maiden
Her thrice-widowed mother; as far as the Rhone
Surpasses the Douro and the Seine the Munda,
The Saone the Sycoris and the Loire the Ebro—
The Loire, the fairest of the streams of France!
So far Amaryllis excels these Spanish nymphs.

Often Melaenis, reflected in the water
Made up her face, painted her eyes, arranged
Her hair—wishing and deserving to seem fair.
And often she said to me, "Silly Daphnis,
What pleasure does it give you if your passion
Rage so long unchecked? Our country, too,
Affords what you desire. Gather the ripe,
The crimson grape, and do not indulge in
Hopes whose fulfilment must be long deferred."
And often Lycisca, passing in the midst
Of a band of revellers, pretending not to look
And turning her face aside, would sing to me
As she danced and beat upon her tambourine:

"The goddess Nemesis is swift to wrath
And her wrath is heavy; Nemesis
Also exacts revenge for injured love.
I have seen a hunter hoping to catch a hare
Reject the hedgehog, and then at evening
Return, his efforts all in vain, with neither
Hare nor hedgehog to take home. I've seen
A fisherman, casting for red mullet,
Throw back the valuable sardine. I've seen
A shepherd who disdained the hollow reeds
That grow on the shore in rows and who preferred
In vain the hard and polished box, at last
(Another having plucked the reeds he scorned)

Content to blow upon a stalk of hemlock.
So it is that Nemesis is wont to
Beat down ostentation out of measure."

Such and so, and more, Melaenis said;
And so, and much, much more Lycisca sung
To me, but always vainly, to deaf ears.
The dog will love the wolf, the bulls love bears,
Hares love foxes or the hind the lioness,
Before Lycisca with her tambourine
Or soft Melaenis cause my love to alter.
The fish must quit the sea, the shades the mountains,
The birds desert the woods, the winds cease sighing,
Before my love for Amaryllis fades.
She has set my heart aflame with such desire
That only her death and mine shall end my love.

NOON

Once powdered angel courtiers with short swords
And red-heeled shoes attended on the Lord's
Levée, to greet the *roi soleil*, who said,
"Sometime remember me when I am dead."
A flutter of wings, of fans ran through the court
Provoking a spiritual lackey to retort,
"As if the bull's eye of the world could die!
Why, has not death been banished from Versailles
And never received here, even in embassy?"

That morning in the *parterre du midi*
Two peasants were apprehended gathering figs,
Male and female. Scandalized, the seraphic periwigs
Soon covered their confusion with a yawn.
Politely through the *parc du Trianon*
A *grand seigneur* escorted them, to show
Them the gates of gilt. They would not take the hint and go
Banned from the artificial wilderness
Till naked amid such shameless fancy dress
And bored by the eternal Sunday, so to speak,
The two turned to the workdays of the week
At last and left, she to spin and he to delve,
As all the clocks in paradise struck twelve.

THE COPPER BEECH

It is half past ten in Stonington.
The trees droop apprehensive of the heat
And the sky has turned that pale suspicious colour
That means that it cannot support more light.
Here on the terrace I and a companion
Each pretends to read. The papers say
That it is 90 in New York today.

Across the street work is going forward
On the abominable house that once I fancied,
Half, might be mine, and which was in fact the home
Of the anonymous couple I used to hear
At night arguing in their unhappy bedroom.
Now they are throwing out another wing
And the site of overlooked love is changed beyond recognition.

What will the day, what will the summer bring?
Psychic storms or calm productive doldrums?
Our neighbours are no saner than ourselves.
Perhaps it is time to give the Stones a ring
Or to complain of the view from the gallery tower
Falling like a shadow across the calm veranda
Rich with malice and the threat of accidental meeting.

This is not a house but a collection
(The largest in private hands?) of sacred objects,
A spiritual boutique where anyone,
Even the wrecker who had come to spoil,
May find himself spending more than he expected
On something he cannot quite identify.
Here the little horrors become the household gods.

For the work of love requires a rule of thumb,
Not no laws in particular but its own
Whose pseudonym, at least here and now, is pleasure:
The morning wasted in work and misquotation,
A light but leisurely lunch, then reading
Walking or just watching the sun all afternoon
Till, hungry, we draw to evening and ombre.

Who are we to thank for all of this?
The greatest favours are conferred in absence
Sometimes, as a syllable gives comfort
Dependent on the time and place and person.
When pleasure and reality occur
Is there room for extra contemplation
Or the lyrical promenade? It is enough

To know (and this is surely recognition)
That the world is spherical and perfect.
Now I wish to introduce the copper beech
We saw on our walk, English and native here as I am,
Whose shade is not the green of contemplation
But the imagination's rich metallic colour
Wherein, under libido, we live.

SONG

Coming back from the beach as from a bath,
Warm and white with the erotic foam
Whence arose the mother of the monthlies,
The wash that all our wishes wander from,
I met youth and beauty in the form
That I can best appreciate: she had a wreathe
Of plastic roses in her hair, and greeted me
With the enchanting salutation, "Hi!"

Purified by salt frivolity,
Bathed in the tidal blood that flows around
The unworthy world, I watched, on my return
The bees that blundered through the underbushes
Of broom and blooming parsley. Suddenly,
As if a chapter opened in my mind,
The air was filled with music: not a note
Disturbed the stillness of the afternoon.

TOTAL IMMERSION

Believe in it? I've seen it done:
The gradual baptism of the moon
Before our eyes in oceanic light,
The sign of an eventual confirmation
When moonlight will become a general condition

Like love or the imagination—not only seen
But known, a phosphorescent tide in life and limb,
The breathing bosom of the starry night,
The splendour and communion of the scene,
A sea of fire in which we naked swim.

THE TROUT

The water my prison shatters in a prism
As I leap alone the dying falls,
Cruel gasps of air, the musical chasm
Intrigue me with their broken intervals.

Deep in the noon of motionless canals
I dreamt away my pale reality
Till stirred by her immortal voice who calls
To the heights of the mountains and the depths of the sea.

I lean on air as prisoners on time
Not to let them down, my impetus
Only to the second hand sublime,
From every point of view ridiculous,

To climb the stair of stone where I was spawned,
Where ponds are oceans and the rapids give
Foretaste of the unbreathable beyond.
I try, I fall, I wriggle loose, I live

Drop by drop against the stream I am,
And in death's little cataract belong
Like Tristan to the torrent and the dam,
Liquid chamber music and still current song,

As I was laid upon the deep sea floor,
Part of the faded pattern of the carpet,
Or spilt like the sperm the kissing fish ignore
Held in each others' scales as in a net.

Yes, I exist, a memory in man
And beast and bird, a universal wish
For the watery world where life began,
And your angelic avatar, the fish:

Ambitious, ghastly, with protuberant eyes,
Or suspended like a living bathysphere,
I negotiate the steps of paradise
Leaping to measures that I cannot hear.

AUGUST 13, 1966

Emerging from the naked labyrinth
Into the golden habit of the day,
Glittering with sweat, a wrestler
With the sun, in his fierce palaestra,

Every drop an angel and a man,
Adept at the being that becomes a man,
You stop before the simple backdrop, look
And listen not to the abstract ocean but to me.

At our backs the breakers serially
Beat a tattoo upon the flat-bellied beach;
In our faces the minutes wait to strike and yawn;
And now the afternoon is nearly gone,
Meanwhile we sit absorbed and precious to each
Other, for the time being where we want to be.

A CONCEIT

Movement alone gives meaning to the view
According to which obnoxious planets turn
Round an incandescent axis. Is it you
Or me for whom the other must rotate and burn?
Earth and sun, we used to be the centre
Each of his own universe, a pivot
Nothing could make wobble. Disorder could not enter
Our too formal gardens, moribund and private.

But experience flat theory disproved.
Now we live in a reciprocal emotion,
Our harmony an interrupted silence,
Our pattern not a treadmill but a dance,
Our being that eternal revolution
By which the sun and other stars are moved.

A VISIT

Le bonheur quel ennui! Mais l'ennui, quel bonheur!

With you the days were scarcely three hours long
Like winter days within the arctic circle
On which a brief and splendid solace shone:
What did we do on which? Let's see, on Monday
We went out, on Tuesday we stayed home
Before the imaginary fire, and read.
From time to time the cat got up and stretched and settled
On a fresh lap, encouraged by our anatomy
To resume the briefly interrupted nap
That is a cat's life. One turned a page.

How slow, how infinitely gentle then
Seemed to us the clumsy flight of time,
Like one of those birds, barnyard or extinct,
That flap from branch to branch but cannot really fly.
Each tick of the clock was noticed, weighed
Like a pulse beat at its proper value.
Thus in no time it was dinner time
And, ah soon after, time to go to bed.

Now I can't remember what we read
Or said, or even how it felt
To have you here, near, within sight and hearing,
Neglected as a treasure is neglected
By its owner, secure in his possession.
Time's deliberate pace, too, was deceptive
For even then in retrospect it flew.

What of the other days, for there were several
Sped in a variety of ways,
Spent like unreplenished capital
To the present starvation of the senses?

On one we took our borrowed bicycles
And followed a path beside the inland sea.
I said, "Is it not like Cornwall or Devon?"
You laughed and replied, "It might be
Were it not for all the ugliness, the highway
Nearby, the brash apartment buildings
And the widespread middle-Western platitude."
Your kind of joke. You observed,
For it was rough, "The waves are wearing mufflers."
If you were a Greek you might have said,
"Underneath, the Nereids are dancing."
And I told you how I used to come
Here alone while waiting for your visit,
In the afternoons, with an apple and a book.

It is painful to remember every morning,
Mornings too intimate almost to record,
Rich and various as a paisley scarf:
You emerging towelled from the bedroom,
And later, together in the shower, masked
In soap, slippery, lascivious as fish.
Too intimate, and yet I keep a record
Of what we did and how and when and where.
Friday you lay back upon the sofa,
Sunday I awoke within your arms,
Thursday you bestrode me like a statue,
And it is as if in all of our embraces
The universal was made personal.

Now: now I need to stop and think a minute.
What have I left out? Oh, everything.
It is like looking at a map of or seeing from the air
A neighbourhood where once one was at home;
Like reading the menu, after, of a meal:
Is it, or in what sense was it, real?

Poets must have something else to write of
Than their own tragic thoughts and epic feelings.
But what? Will a comic interruption do?
The scramble, worthy of a bedroom farce,
When the delivery boy rang the bell, the sudden
Sinister breakdown of the telephone,
Which now, like my anxiety, seems funny.
Or your silent tears? The stories of the resistance
In which you shone with an ironic virtue
Maladroit, touchingly inferior, and wise?

The very muchness of the world disgusts me
Some times, when it comes between us two,
And suddenly I lose all appetite.
At others it is all we have together:
Like the moments on the bus, to me terrific
(You never guessed with what courage taken)
Before we said goodbye again. You proved then
How much can be included in a look,
And the fleeting sun illuminated
As it set the shining fancy of your flesh.

UNTITLED

Here is another poem in a picture:

at the end of the gallery, so you will see them as
you enter, Christ Crucified, the Virgin and Saint
John, attributed to a famous Flemish master.

The attribution of guilt is universal.

There is something distinctly fishy about these figures.
Literally. Streamlined and coldblooded. As weightless
as a fish might feel in water. The man of sorrows not
nailed to his cross but pinned there. Almost as if he
had no body. Nobody to suffer and depend on. No body
to depend on wood and iron and to suffer. Which heresy
pretended he did not? Nonetheless he suffers obviously,
enthroned on his gibbet, naked and erect as if he held
it up.

His mother, fainting in the arms of the disciple Jesus
loved, will never in the conceivable future fall to
earth. And this in spite of the gingerly way he holds
her as he leans slightly forward on tiptoe, his fingers
parted and outstretched as if to seize the air. His
tentative, mimic gesture of support. He does not grasp
at anything. There is no strain or effort apparent
anywhere in the composition.

She sinks down as if onto a chair, stricken by grief,
sustained in theory by love. Her hands are clasped,
her eyes are almost closed. And beneath the smooth
expressive drapery one has to infer the insubstantial
flesh. Goodness! one exclaims, What painting, a
craft in the radical sense pretentious, to suggest
what is equivocally there.

Each wears the appropriate expression like an honorary
degree: he an anthropomorphic mask of pity, she
negligently the distinction of her tears. Only the
saviour of their world wears nothing except a difficult
crown of thorns which hurts.

The cause of their distress is unconcerned. They
do not look upon him as their redeemer as yet, but
as a son and dear friend whose eccentricities have
got him into trouble. One can forgive too many and
love too much.

The birth and banquet of love look equally far away
and insignificant from here; the resurrection is also
inconceivable. Only the ignominious and painful
moment of death has any meaning now, a meaning
without a future or a past.

The background is conventional, a wall too high to
see over, too smooth to climb, draped here and there
with a red linen cloth, its folds still visible.

Beyond the wall there is a gold leaf sky.

Remember that everything is possible,
The picture, the poem and ourselves,
The blood that we see shed, the tears that we
Shed, the wall, and the anonymous cross.

POINT GREY

Brought up as I was to ask of the weather
Whether it was fair or overcast,
Here, at least, it is a pretty morning,
The first fine day as I am told in months.
I took a path that led down to the beach,
Reflecting as I went on landscape, sex and weather.

I met a welcome wonderful enough
To exorcise the educated ghost
Within me. No, this country is not haunted,
Only the rain makes spectres of the mountains.

There they are, and there somehow is the problem
Not exactly of freedom or of generation
But just of living and the pain it causes.
Sometimes I think the air we breathe is mortal
And dies, trapped, in our unfeeling lungs.

Not too distant the mountains and the morning
Dropped their dim approval on the gesture
With which enthralled I greeted all this grandeur.
Beside the path, half buried in the bracken,
Stood a long-abandoned concrete bunker,
A little temple of lust, its rough walls covered
With religious frieze and votary inscription.

Personally I know no one who doesn't suffer
Some sore of guilt, and mostly bedsores, too,
Those that come from itching where it scratches
And that dangerous sympathy called prurience.
But all about release and absolution
Lie, in the waves that lap the dirty shingle
And the mountains that rise at hand above the rain.
Though I had forgotten that it could be so simple,
A beauty of sorts is nearly always within reach.

TERMINAL CONVERSATION

Born to return to every strange new place,
Seeing, as the Buddha says, that you only live once,
I found myself in a great railway station
After midnight. That was late enough for me,
Though anyone who was everyone was there.
Blank terminus or furnished house? For, strange to say,
The waiting room had all the furniture of home.

It was winter, the last train had gone.
You will recognize the *mise en scène*
Familiar from too many foreign movies.
Those beside me showed no signs of caring,
And it was plain they thought of going nowhere
At that hour of the night or, already, morning.
They settled down, resident aliens,
To what they appeared to accept as the human condition,
To sleep and not to read, or to discussion
Of the trivia of their uprooted lives
In a language that, although it was not mine,
I found at once that I could understand.

What they were saying in that foreign tongue:

That emotions should be christened for their object
And not abstractly for their content. Fear and love
Would become *a certain danger* or just *you*.
Perhaps, somebody suggested, we should point
And thus avoid misunderstanding and the ills
That generally come from saying what one means.
There was a school of thought in opposition
Of course—there always is—which said
That the old names were best and meant just what they said.

Nearby some people were discussing nothing.
As far as I recall their conversation,
Some maintained that nothingness was zero
Or at least that they conceived it so,
While certain others insisted that they felt
The absence of sensation as a lack,
A positive negation, so to speak,
Dissatisfaction, disappearance, disillusion
Or even the destruction of the object,
And said that nothing equalled minus one.

All about the furniture stood, dumb,
The most expressive that I ever saw,
It had the grateful look of having been
Rescued from oblivion: those chairs
Had lived in disgrace underground for years,
And that inlaid table, too, an exile
Returned from somebody's attic déclassé
In company with the out of tune piano
And a distinctly down at heels *duchesse*.

As for the lamps: every one had started
Life as something other than a lamp,
As a typewriter, a trumpet or a doll,
And been converted, willy nilly lucifer.
Who put them there? What stranded housewife furnished
This most impersonal of places
With the heirlooms of her private fancy,
Or did I dream that they and I were there?

The station clock was keeping public time
Above our heads. A janitor
Who might have been the janitor of nowhere
Pushed his broom across the mottled pavement
Gathering cigarette ends, newspapers,
The dated detritus of a sleepless night
Into a canvas bag. I yawned, I yawn
Remembering the meaninglessness now,
The empty hours and uncomfortable faces,
The marble and mysterious conversation,
The out of place old fashioned furniture
And my secret sense that this was, where I was,
A haven however strange however new.

A PRESENT

Spring is late and I am going blind.
In his dark room my neighbour draws the blind
In order to develop. What? A film
Taken last summer. Underneath the chemical film
Of free association our features are still bright.
"Bruno wasn't really very bright,"
I write in my commonplace book, and pour myself a drink.
This winter is interminable. I drink
Too much. My neighbour doesn't drink at all.
But in his dark room he will work all
Night, developing the past.
I think of the future chronically, of the past
On occasion; never, never of the present.
Each day, cold and dimmer, is like a birthday present.

THE SURVIVORS

Nowadays the mess is everywhere
And getting worse. Earth after all
Is a battlefield. Through the static
We used to call the music of the spheres

Someone, a survivor, sends this message:
"When it happened I was reading Homer.
Sing—will nobody sing?—the wrath,
Rats and tanks and radioactive rain."

That was before rationing was enforced
On words, of course. Particles went first,
Then substantives. Now only verbs abide
The law, and the odd anarchistic scrawl

How above the crumbling horizon
Brightly shine our neighbours, Venus, Mars.

FAREWELL TO THE POINT

On the popular beach heaps of unwanted fish
Which the lake can't support, rotten, instruct the sense:
Goodness, death is obscene! Decently smell of grass
New mown masks an unfresh, dreadfully human smell—
Our flesh, frequently oiled, candidly bare, and now
Burnt the colour of earth. Death is no prude: we stink.
Bodies litter this be-in like a day of wrath
Where all flesh is as grass under the influence
Of the sun as a great harvester. Shiny-new,
Far superior to our obsolescent kind,
Winged, inhuman (although somebody thought it up)
Bare-war-headed, the U 2, perhaps phoney too,
Nicknamed Niké, the dike goddess of victory
(Whose, we aren't to decide), casts a tumescent, rude
Shadow over the ripe, lazy, unwilling scene.
This is It against which, being, we demonstrate—
Or, like Beauty, should we thank it for being there
Tipped with nervous antennae like a lightning bug
Or tin-horned blatant beast groping horizons for
Love objects to destroy? Some supersonic fears
Subside under the crude blaze of the umpty-watt
Bulb up there. We become natural creatures, eat,
Drink and pray and protest. This is our way of life
As, existing, we dread less the untidy dark
That we cannot postpone, no, not another wink.
Blank sun swung on a cord, pealing, distempered sky,
Beauty spots like a plague dot over heaven's face,
Horsemen sweeping across Eden and violet
Air: the signs of a soon, apocalyptic storm
Coming after the gross, uninterrupted calm,
Pleasure's principle suppressed, overthrown by force,
Void the castle of sense, being itself suspect,
Phantasy undermined, all that we call the real
Gone, we wake from a dream threatening war for love:

Rocket, destitute fish, flesh; and our slogans spell
Nonsense syllables, hip, meaningless after all.

TABLEAU VIVANT

Perseus on an ornamental charger,
German work, sixteenth century,
Hovering above the slumbering Medusa
Like a buzzing fly or a mosquito
On beaten, golden wings. His head averted
From her agate gaze. In his right hand
A sword, in his left a mirror.

Helmeted by night, slipshod by darkness.
Wondering where to strike. She looks asleep
As if dreaming of petrified forests,
Monumental dryads, stone leaves, stone limbs,
Or of the mate that she will never meet
Who will look into her eyes and live.

LOVERS OF THE RIVER

Hell's Gate is hot, a hundred degrees at Hope.
Then as we descend the infernal canyon
The cleft between its walls grows smaller,
The blank or smiling faces near the top
Indistinct, the hot rocks are dotted here and there
With pine trees like a growth of private
Hair, while curling at the bottom
The patient and inconsequential river
Flows as it will flow forever
Approximately
Always a deeper pathway to the sea.

This chasm is important to the eye
But tricky, a place of fissures
And lapses fatal in the winter.
At all times of the year it is better to go slowly
And keep together, for fear of rattlesnakes,
Getting lost, sunstroke and tedium,
Wahlverwandschaften,
For far away the furthest trading post.

These traditionally are the lovers of the river,
Bearded men, uxorious fur trappers,
Voyageurs and wicked red skin guides,
Children who lost their childhood to the river,
Unfrocked priests and frivolous runaways
Who love without responsibility,
Men with nothing but their proper
Masculinity,
In theory the half of human kind.

Where at nightfall do they make their camp?
Where are the drunken springs of inspiration?
Leafless groves of fir and spruce and cedar?
In glacial streams and lakes they bathe their bodies'
Hardihood,
In sunstruck meadows rest.

And live and die in spite of one another.
The myth is not unnatural to them
How one descending from the precipice,
A rope about his waist, discovered
His comrade dead and rescue come too late.
Unnatural are the newly rich motels
Superb highways and the love of women
That always go with easy money,
Meretriciousness
Afflicting every scenic calendar.

They love the river not in its beginnings
Nor its anticlimax in the sea,
They love it in the middle of its journey,
The difficult stretches after it emerges
From underground caverns that are none of their business,
And watch its abrupt waterfalls and rapids
And care as guardians should impartially
For all the tributaries that supply it, the
Distillation
Of glacier and spring.

Only they and we lose interest
When certain sandbars past it spreads and coarsens,
Matures in fact to feed a growing valley
Offering its banks to trees and cattle
And eventually to wharfs and mills and learns
To bear the busy burdens of the world.

They do not care as we have come to care for harbours.
They love the river as an adolescent
And remember, growing old in estuaries,
Fondly,
How rough and clear and small and cold it was.

AMONG ISLANDS

Fratrum quoque gratia rara est. OVID *Met.* I 145

The ferry is at home among the islands
On which it calls at blessed intervals,
We are exiles everywhere we go,
Stranded upon the veranda, castaways
In the family living room, like Crusoe,
Or like Philoctetes, festering,
Having given away the Herculean bow,
With nothing to call our own except the wound.

If this is true and universal, what of you
Who disembark upon familiar landings
As an islander moving among islands,
Businesslike, unaltered by the view
And knowing what comes next, so the horizon
Has nothing strange to offer, nothing new?

Natural where I am affected
And strangely moved by the very names of islands.
My pen shakes and destroys their capitals,
They sink beneath the strokes of the Waterman
And from the waves of scripture rise again,
Pender, Saltspring, Thetis, Galiano,
Created as the Word was out of nothing.

Not created either but begotten,
And not as you and I were, namelessly
In haste and shame, as we imagine, neither
Knowing who our only begetters were
Except that they are like two floating islands
That clashed perhaps in ecstasy and parted
Leaving behind a continent of self.
But for this fact or act which we infer,
Of which we are ourselves the inference,
You and I know nothing of our sowing.

Knowing thereby no less than many know
Growing up in ignorance, ignoring
Even the awkward grace they do not know.
Only he whose lover lost the islands
Boasted he did not know, and all the knowledge
Worth having since then has been that we know nothing.

Which has its advantages. You can do anything
With that which you do not know, what you possess
Like the gifts of the gods, unknowing. Islands,
Sunny, south, pacific islands float
Upon a cloudy sea of ignorance;
And that mysterious love which has given us
Everything asks nothing in return.

So welcome, brother, to the fabled islands
Of the blessed, which you shall inhabit
Hopefully for unending summer
Days that know nothing of age, inflation, death.

And welcome to the world, a thousand islands
Each persuaded of its own uniqueness
And unsuspecting nothing is its name.

That August afternoon you told me nothing
And I asked you no questions, figuring
After all the summer said it all.
We respected the fiction of each other's names,
Leaning in a fraternal silence on
The railing of the ferry, guest, companion
Side by side, cruising among islands.

THE NAP

. . . and with the wingéd boy
Sporting himself in safe felicity:
Who when he hath with spoils and cruelty
Ransack'd the world, and in the woful hearts
Of many wretches set his triumphs high,
Thither resorts, and laying his sad darts
Aside, with fair Adonis plays his wanton parts.
SPENSER, *The Faerie Queen*, II, vi, 49

My wristwatch tells me that we've had a little nap.
    Perhaps it's stopped meantime? No, it goes,
Ticks and moves its minute hand. Upon my lap
    Catullus and *Daniel Deronda* doze.
Dreamer and reader equally, I fear to wake and snap
    The thread of their intelligent repose.
The china tea in the cup beside me is quite cold.
    Quite cold, the two extremities I hold.

With the precision of assassins the hands of the clock have crept
    Stealthily to quarter after two,
In spite of which I am unsure how long we've slept
    (For cat and book must both sleep when I do),
Nor can I remember what I was dreaming about, except
    That once again I know I dreamt of you,
Ashamed of my furtive affection, thanking the disgrace
    Of sleep wherein you have your hiding place.

No less place, to be sure, have you in waking thought,
    But there you are less vivid and you share
Their conscious character and over-complex plot
    With narratives to which you can't compare.
Exquisite structure! your doings are with such meaning fraught
    As Reason dreamt of in her *Dictionnaire*.
Awake I try your face and cannot get it clear,
    Asleep I see and touch and taste and hear.

So very near in dreams the naked body, nice
    Even when armed, and like a shield, and white;
Dark the pudenda in the midst like a device,
    The badge of bliss and blazon of delight.
There Eros practises his plays in paradise
    And member-loving Aphrodite might
Be to her Adonis for a second what she seems
    In the hall of night and hospital of dreams.

For ought I not to know the signs of the disease
    By now: what I don't have and what you are?
And see the diagnosis confirmed as it agrees
    With every previous wound and precious scar?
Fever at first is thrilling, it never fails to please,
    Only slowly do the symptoms become peculiar.
Illness is idiosyncratic: healthier to ignore
    The fact in favour of the metaphor.

Whatever science does the experiment succumbs,
    Its tools are deadly, dexterous and deep.
Each local anaesthetic altogether numbs.
    I sigh for love's suppository sleep.
Out of dismemberment the unconscious comes
    Awake to take its medicine and weep.
The dear physician does the necessary, sings
    A measure, pleasure's overture: it stings.

Antaeus when once separated from the ground
    Relaxed within the grasp of Heracles.
Above the earth he sought his mastery and found
    That he could conquer only on his knees;
As we by the laws of gravity too bound
    Savour the aftertaste of victories
In which like children caught up and tossed in sport
    We for a moment flew without support:

Until the firm familiar arms of fantasy
  Turn transparent as the windowpane,
And you as one of those, perhaps, appear to me,
  Impromptu pieces that I rehearse again
With sad darts of wit and wanton apology.
  Suddenly I feel I am in pain.
You go, I wake, Catullus stretches, everything
  Vanishes backwards, love and suffering.

DARYL HINE

Daryl Hine was born in British Columbia, Canada,
in 1936. He studied Classics and Philosophy at
McGill University in Montreal. In 1968 he was
awarded a Canada Council (Rockefeller) Award for
poetry, and went abroad; in 1959 he received a Canada
Council Grant. He lived principally in France until
1962, when he returned to this continent, first, briefly
to New York, where he worked as a free lance poetry
editor, and then, in 1963, to the University of Chicago,
where he resumed his studies, taking first an M.A.
then a Ph.D. in Comparative Literature. The subject
of his doctoral thesis was the Latin poetry of George
Buchanan, the sixteenth century Scottish humanist.
In 1967 he joined the faculty of the University of
Chicago, where he teaches writing and comparative
literature.
He has published five collections of his poetry; a novel
(*The Prince of Darkness and Co.*, 1961), and a travel
book (*Polish Subtitles*, 1962). He has had several plays,
including a verse translation of Euripides' *Alcestis*,
produced on the Canadian Broadcasting Corporation
and the British Broadcasting Corporation's Third
Programme. His latest play, *The Death of Seneca* was
given a dramatic reading during the University
of Chicago's Liberal Arts Conference, and will be
published in a forthcoming issue of the *Chicago Review*.